The Pelican Brief

JOHN GRISHAM

Level 5

Retold by Robin Waterfield
Series Editors: Andy Hopkins and Jocelyn Potter

Pearson Education Limited
Edinburgh Gate, Harlow,
Essex CM20 2JE, England
and Associated Companies throughout the world.

ISBN 0 582 41796 1

First published in the United Kingdom by Century Ltd 1992
This adaptation first published by Penguin Books 1995
Published by Addison Wesley Longman Limited and Penguin Books Ltd. 1998
New edition first published 1999

Second impression 2000

Text copyright © Robin Waterfield 1995
Illustrations copyright © Rowan Clifford 1995
All rights reserved

The moral right of the adapter and of the illustrator has been asserted

Typeset by RefineCatch Limited, Bungay, Suffolk
Set in 11/14pt Monotype Bembo
Printed in Spain by Mateu Cromo, S.A. Pinto (Madrid)

Published by Pearson Education Limited in association with
Penguin Books Ltd., both companies being subsidiaries of Pearson Plc

For a complete list of the titles available in the Penguin Readers series please write to your local
Pearson Education office or to: Marketing Department, Penguin Longman Publishing,
5 Bentinck Street, London W1M 5RN.

Contents

Introduction

'My best friend is dead because of the Pelican Brief,' Gavin said. 'He was killed by a car bomb. Someone is worried . . . don't you think?'

The Supreme Court is the highest court in the United States. Its nine judges are some of the most important people in the country. One day in October, two are found dead.

It is a professional job. No one can find any answers – no connection between the two, no reason for the deaths.

But, while the FBI and the President argue it out between them, a young law student goes to work. And soon Darby Shaw knows more than anyone, enough to name names – enough to frighten *someone* badly. Enough to make them want to kill her.

It's hard for a beautiful woman to hide. But she has to stay alive. She has to tell someone what she knows.

The Pelican Brief is John Grisham's third novel and a number one best-seller throughout the world. In its first year on sale over five million copies were printed in the United States.

John Grisham is now widely considered to be the world's number one best-selling author. He was born in 1955 in Arkansas, in the United States. Though his family were poor, he went to Mississippi State University and later started his own law firm. He started to write in 1984 and his first book was *A Time to Kill*. Though this was not successful at first, he sold his next book, *The Firm*, for $200,000 and the film rights for $600,000. He gave up his law practice immediately. He now owns a large farm in Mississippi, where he lives with his wife and two children in a specially built Victorian-style house.

The Pelican Brief was a successful film in 1993, with Julia Roberts as Darby Shaw.

Chapter 1   Three Bodies

The man who was waiting on the shore looked like a farmer. He wore the right kind of clothes, and his van, which was parked on the dirt road above the beach, was suitably covered in mud.

It was midnight on the first Monday in October, and for the next thirty minutes he had to wait there. He stared out to sea. He was alone, as he knew he would be; it was planned that way. This beach was always empty at this time of night. No cars drove along the dirt road.

The clouds were low and thick. It would be difficult to see the boat until it was close. That was planned as well.

After he had waited twenty minutes he heard the sound of a quiet engine from the water and then saw a black rubber boat, low in the water, approach the shore. The engine stopped when the boat was about thirty feet from the shore. The farmer looked around. There were no people, no cars.

He carefully put a cigarette in his mouth and started to smoke it. A man's voice came from the boat on the water: 'What kind of cigarette is that?'

'Lucky Strike,' the farmer answered.

Satisfied, the man in the boat asked, 'Luke?'

'Sam,' replied the farmer. The man in the boat was Khamel, not Sam, and Luke knew it.

Luke had often heard of Khamel, but he was not sure that they had met before. Khamel had many names and many faces, and he spoke several languages. He was the most famous and most feared killer in the world. He was the best. At first, twenty years ago, he had killed for political reasons, but now he would kill anyone, anywhere, if the money was right.

1

Luke was excited. Khamel was going to be working in America. He wondered who was going to die. Whoever it was, the killing would be quick and clean, and there would be no clues.

At dawn, the stolen van stopped at a hotel in Georgetown, part of Washington, DC, the political capital of the United States of America. Khamel got out of the van without a word to Luke. They had not spoken throughout the journey, and Luke had been careful not to look at Khamel. He didn't want to die; he didn't want Khamel to think he could recognize him.

The room in the hotel was ready, of course. The curtains were tightly closed. The car keys were on the table. The gun was in a briefcase next to the bed.

He had received three million dollars already for this job. He would phone his bank in three hours to ask whether the next four million had arrived. While he waited, he practised his English in front of the mirror. The job would be over by midnight tonight, so another three million would reach his bank by midday tomorrow. By then he would be in Paris. It was satisfactory. He allowed himself a short sleep.

◆

The Supreme Court is the highest court in the USA. It consists of nine judges, who hear only the most difficult cases in the country – those cases which might actually threaten the Constitution. Judges are appointed to the Supreme Court by the government, so a Republican government will try to get Republican judges appointed and a Democratic government will try to get Democrats appointed.★ Judges become members of the Supreme Court for life. They can retire if they want, but if

★ Republicans and Democrats: the two main political sides in the USA.

not the job ends only with death. Judge Rosenberg was so old that he found it hard to stay awake sometimes, even during trials. He was a liberal, and proud of it. He defended the Indians, the homosexuals, the poor, the blacks, the Mexicans and the Puerto Ricans. Some people loved him for it, but more people hated him.

Throughout the summer there had been the usual number of messages threatening death to the judges of the Supreme Court, and as usual Rosenberg had received more than the others. The FBI had to behave as if the judges really were in danger, although they were threatened year after year and it was very rare for anything to happen. When it did, it was usually a single madman, whose daughter had died in a road accident or something. The political groups made a lot of noise, but it was easier for them to bomb buildings than people, and especially people who were as well guarded as the Supreme Court judges.

Rosenberg refused to have FBI guards in his own home; he had lived to be ninety-one and was not afraid of death. Judge Jensen had different reasons for not wanting guards in his house: he wanted to be able to come and go as he pleased. Both of them allowed the guards to wait outside, in cars or on foot, but they could enter the house only when they had permission.

◆

A little after ten at night, when the house was dark and still, the door to a bedroom cupboard opened and Khamel came quietly out. He was dressed in running clothes. He had shaved off his beard and coloured his hair blond.

Silently, he went down the stairs. He knew there were two FBI men in a car that was parked on the road outside the front of the house; he knew there was another guard, Ferguson, walking around the house outside.

Rosenberg and his male nurse were asleep in the downstairs bedroom. Outside the door, Khamel fitted a silencer on to his gun. He stepped inside, put the gun to the head of the nurse and fired three times. The hands and legs jumped, but the eyes stayed closed, and there was no sound. Khamel quickly reached across to the grey old head of Judge Rosenberg and shot three bullets into it.

He watched the two bodies for a full minute, and then went out to the kitchen. He opened the back door, waited until Ferguson appeared in the back garden, and then called his name. He knew that the nurse often invited Ferguson in for a cup of coffee and something to eat.

Ferguson obediently came into the kitchen. Khamel fired three bullets into the back of his head and he fell loudly on to the table. Khamel left the gun there and went out of the back door. As soon as he reached the road at the back of the house, he began running. He was just another American, out for his nightly run.

♦

In the dark of the Montrose Theatre, Glenn Jensen sat by himself and watched the men on the big screen in the front of the theatre. He was dressed in ordinary clothes – clothes that no one would remember – and wore dark glasses too. Nobody would know that he had been here. He came to this homosexual film theatre once or twice a week, and not even his FBI guards knew about it.

It was easy to get out of the house. There were several apartments in the building, and the two FBI men could watch only one entrance at a time. All he had to do was change his clothes and drive away in a friend's car. He liked the Montrose because the films went on all night and there was never a crowd. Tonight there were only two old men, sitting together

4

Khamel quickly reached across to the grey old head of Judge Rosenberg and shot three bullets into it.

in the middle of the theatre and holding hands. Jensen watched their backs and wondered if he would be like them in twenty years. At forty-four, he was the youngest of the Supreme Court judges.

He was not a favourite of either the Republicans or the Democrats, but had been a safe appointment for the Republican President four years ago. He was not particularly liberal, except in cases involving homosexuals and those where industry threatened the environment. He usually tried to judge his cases according to their rights and wrongs, rather than any political opinions.

A fourth person entered the theatre where Jensen and the two old men were now enjoying a film in which several young men were in bed together. He wore tight jeans, a black shirt, an earring, dark glasses and a moustache. Khamel the homosexual. He smiled when he saw Jensen there. The information they had given him was good.

At 12:20 the old men left the theatre, arm in arm. Jensen did not look at them; he was too busy watching the film. Khamel moved like a cat to a seat behind Jensen. He pulled some rope from round his waist and wrapped the ends round his hands. He suddenly put the rope around the front of Jensen's neck and pulled backwards and downwards. Jensen's neck broke over the back of his seat. Just to make sure, Khamel twisted the rope until it bit deeply into Jensen's neck and held it there for two minutes.

An hour later he was waiting at Dulles airport for his flight to Paris.

Chapter 2   Political Planning

The phone woke the President at 4:30 in the morning. He listened to the voice for a minute and then jumped out of bed. Eight minutes later he was in the office. Fletcher Coal, his chief of staff, was waiting for him.

'What the hell happened?' the President asked.

Coal walked up and down in front of the President's desk. 'We don't know much,' he said. 'They're both dead. Two FBI men found Rosenberg at one a.m. His nurse and guard were also dead. Three bullets each – very clean, very professional. While the FBI were at Rosenberg's house, they heard that the police had found Jensen's body in a homosexual club. Voyles called me, and I called you. He'll be here in a minute.'

'Rosenberg is dead,' the President said.

'Yes. At last.' Rosenberg and the Republican Government had not been friends. 'I suggest you go on TV in two or three hours' time and tell the country about it all. Mabry is already working on your speech. We don't want to leave it until later, because we want to be the first to tell them. The press already have the news.'

'I didn't know he was a homosexual.'

'There's no doubt about it now. This is the perfect crisis. We didn't cause it; we didn't do anything wrong. The country will be shocked and they'll turn to you. You're going to be more popular than ever, and next year you'll be elected again for another four years. It's great.'

'And I can get two new men into the Supreme Court.'

'Exactly. That's the best bit. They'll be your men, and they'll be there for ever. You'll have a first list of names by tomorrow.'

'Are there any suspects?'

'Not yet.'

The President smiled. 'Voyles's FBI men were supposed to protect the judges, weren't they? Good. I want you to leak that information to the press. Maybe we can get rid of Voyles too.'

When Voyles arrived a moment later, the President and Coal tried to look worried. Voyles told them that there were no suspects yet, and the President asked for a list by five o'clock that evening. They agreed that the killings must be connected. Voyles denied that his men had been careless.

'Rosenberg and Jensen are dead because they refused to let us guard them properly,' he said. 'We're guarding the other seven, and they're still alive.'

'At the moment,' the President said, and looked at Coal. They almost smiled. They could easily make Voyles look stupid and inefficient over this business. Voyles knew it too. He was going to have to be careful. The President – or rather Coal, who told the President what to think – wanted his head, and the press would eat him alive. Back in his office, he ordered a full enquiry into the murders.

◆

Darby Shaw woke up a little before dawn. After fifteen months of law school at Tulane University in New Orleans, her mind refused to rest for more than six hours. The work had not been so hard at her first university, in Phoenix, Arizona, where she had specialized in environmental science. Then she decided to become a lawyer and to defend the environment in the courts. The price was hard work and more hard work.

There were some rewards, however. She turned over in the bed to look at the man sleeping next to her. Thomas Callahan was one of the most popular teachers in the university. He was forty-five years old, but seemed a lot younger. He drank a lot, wore jeans, drove a Porsche, lived in the French Quarter and managed to make even constitutional law interesting. He was also good in bed. And for the first time in his life he had stayed with one woman for more than a few weeks. Darby and he had been together now for several months. She smiled and wondered what her fellow students would think. Only her very best friends knew the secret.

She turned the TV on and suddenly there was the President. She listened for a minute and then shook Thomas awake. 'Thomas! Wake up! Listen to this!' She turned the sound up louder.

Callahan sat up and stared at the screen, still half asleep. He understood what the President was saying, though. 'Rosenberg? Murdered?' he said. Darby knew that Rosenberg was his hero.

'Jensen too,' she said.

The President finished his speech and Darby switched the TV off.

'No suspects, according to the President,' Callahan said.

'I can think of at least twenty groups who wanted Rosenberg dead,' Darby said, 'starting with the Ku-Klux-Klan.'*

'Yeah, but why those two judges? OK, lots of people wanted Rosenberg dead, but why Jensen? Why not McDowell or Yount? They're both more liberal than Jensen.'

'Maybe they both just got killed on the same night by chance,' Darby suggested, without believing it.

'No, I don't think so,' said Callahan. 'These are the first Supreme Court judges ever to be murdered – and then two in one night? There must be some connection between the murders. But you know the worst thing? That fool President will

* The Ku-Klux-Klan is a political group in the USA which believes that white people are better than black people.

9

be able to fill their places. That means that eight out of the nine will be Republicans. We won't be able to recognize the Constitution in ten years. This is awful.'

'Perhaps that's why they were killed, Thomas. Someone or some group wants a different Supreme Court, filled with Republicans.'

'But why Jensen? He was appointed by a Republican.'

'I don't know, but there must be some connection. Maybe there's a clue in the cases the Supreme Court was due to hear this year. The library will have that information. I think I'll spend some time on this today.'

Chapter 3   No Clues

Denton Voyles put Eric East in charge of the case. On Thursday, East reported back to Voyles with a list of their top suspects. There were a number of political groups – especially the Underground Army, the Ku-Klux-Klan and the White Defenders – but also some individuals who were rich enough to afford the kind of professional killer who had obviously done this job. There was Nelson Muncie, who had lost his daughter in a sex killing in Florida; the police had caught the man, who was black, but thanks to Rosenberg the man had walked free. There was Clinton Lane, whose son was a homosexual who had died of Aids. The problem with all these suspects, however, was that the killings were so professional and clean that there were no clues except for the gun and the rope. There were not even any clues about how the killer had entered Rosenberg's house. Still, Voyles and he agreed to have between five and twenty men investigate each suspect or group of suspects.

In the law library and on the computers of Tulane University, Darby Shaw was gathering pages and pages of information.

What was the connection between Rosenberg and Jensen? She could see reasons for killing one or the other, but not both together. But there had to be a single reason.

◆

Thomas Callahan slept late and alone. Darby had been too busy to see him since Wednesday. Now it was Friday morning. He made some coffee and, as he drank it, watched the busy French Quarter through his window.

What was it he had to do? Oh, yes, phone Gavin. On Monday he was going to Washington for a conference about constitutional law. He and his old friend Gavin Verheek were going to meet and get drunk together on Monday evening. Gavin had been a friend ever since law school. He and Callahan were the only two in their year who refused to go into private practice and get rich. While Callahan had become a teacher, Verheek had joined the FBI as a legal adviser.

When Verheek came on the phone, he said, 'Thomas, how are you?'

'It's ten-thirty. I'm not dressed. I'm sitting here in the French Quarter drinking coffee and watching the world outside. What are you doing?'

'Well, here it's eleven-thirty, and I haven't left the office since they found the bodies on Wednesday morning.'

'It makes me sick, Gavin. The President will get two Nazis on to the Supreme Court. I suppose you've already seen the list. I bet your office is already checking that they've lived good, clean lives. Go on, Gavin, tell me who's on the list. I won't tell anyone else.'

'No chance. I'll only tell you this: your name's not on the list.'

'I'm so disappointed.'

'How's the girl?'

'Which one?'

'Come on, Thomas. The girl?'

'She's beautiful and brilliant and gentle. Oh, and rich. She has red hair and the longest legs you've ever seen.'

'Wow! What's her name?'

'Darby Shaw. But I haven't seen her for a couple of days. She's trying to solve the murders all by herself. Why don't you tell me who did it, and then I can tell her and she'll come back to me?'

'Don't you read the papers? We have no suspects. Not one.'

'At least I tried. Are we going to meet on Monday?'

'I hope so. Voyles wants us to work day and night until the computers tell us who did it.'

'I'll expect a full report on Monday, Gavin – not just the gossip.'

'Why don't you bring Darby? How old is she? Nineteen?'

'Twenty-four, and she's not invited. I'll see you on Monday at seven p.m., in the usual restaurant. OK?'

'OK. See you.'

◆

Darby's enquiries had brought her to the court in Lafayette. Of all the Supreme Court cases due to be heard in the next few months, there was one that could explain the killings. She needed to see the court's files on the case. When the clerk brought them to her table, however, her heart sank. There were lots of files, each inches thick. The case was seven years old. Only one person was involved, but he had hidden behind thirty-eight different businesses, which had used no fewer than fifteen law firms over the last seven years.

She pulled her chair in to the table and began to work.

Chapter 4   Ideas and Information

The meeting East and Voyles had with Coal and the President did not go well. Not only could they not report any progress, but they had to admit that investigations like this could take many months.

Then Coal handed Voyles a list of eight possible members of the Supreme Court, two of whom would fill the places left empty by Rosenberg and Jensen. 'We want a report on these people in ten days, Voyles,' he said, 'and make sure the press doesn't get to hear about them.'

'You know we can't promise that,' Voyles said. 'We can't guarantee no leaks. As soon as we start to dig around these people, someone will realize what's going on.'

'The FBI can't guarantee secrecy?' Coal said. 'You'd better keep this out of the papers, Voyles.'

Voyles jumped out of his chair. 'Listen, Coal,' he shouted. 'Why don't you investigate these people yourself? Don't start telling me what to do.'

The President tried to make peace. 'All we're saying is do your best, Voyles,' he said. 'These people are young and they're good Republicans. They'll be giving the Constitution shape long after I'm dead. So it's important to me that the two who become members of the Supreme Court are clean, so that they can stay there for ever. So no drugs, no unusual sexual habits – nothing like that. OK?'

'Yes, Mr President. But we cannot guarantee total secrecy.'

'I understand. Just try your best.'

'Yes, sir.'

◆

Callahan went round to Darby's apartment with a pizza and a bottle of wine. He hadn't seen her for four days. He rang on her doorbell.

*Coal handed Voyles a list of eight possible members
of the Supreme Court.*

'Who is it?' she called through the door.

'Thomas Callahan,' he said. 'Do you remember me?'

The door opened and Callahan stepped in. 'Are we still friends?' he asked, and gave her a kiss.

'Of course. I've just been busy.'

'So what did the great detective find?'

She was opening the bottle of wine and didn't answer straight away. She poured wine into two glasses and they went and sat together on the sofa. She put her legs up on to him, and he stroked them. He repeated the question.

'Nothing, really. I was following a path, and it took me somewhere. I even typed it up as a brief, but I don't think it's worth anything.'

'What? You've been running around playing detective for four days, and refusing to see me, and now you're just going to throw it away?'

'It's over there on the table, if you want to see it,' she said.

'I don't want to see it now,' he said. 'We have more important things to do. I'm going to be away in Washington for a few days, remember? I'll read your brief and then we'll talk about it. But not till we've been to bed, OK?'

She pulled him towards her and they kissed long and hard.

◆

There was a cleaner in the White House whom everyone called Sarge. He was old, very black, and had white hair. He wore dark glasses all the time, and everyone thought that he was half blind.

In fact, Sarge could see very well. He could see round corners. He had been working in the White House for thirty years now, cleaning and listening, cleaning and seeing. He knew which doors stayed open and which walls were thin. No one ever noticed him.

His son Cleve was a policeman. This is how it worked: Cleve would contact Gray Grantham of the *Washington Post* and arrange a meeting. Sarge and Grantham would meet. No one knew how Grantham got his political information, but it was always good and always correct. Sarge never talked to anyone except Grantham, and he didn't tell even him everything he found out.

This time they met at Glenda's, a little café on Fourteenth Street. Sarge was able to tell Grantham two of the people on the list of possible Supreme Court judges.

Chapter 5   An Implausible Theory

Verheek had drunk too much the night before with Callahan, as he had known he would. What had he said? Had he given away any secrets? He remembered explaining that the connection between Rosenberg and Jensen was not political. The connection was so obvious that for several days no one in the FBI had seen it. They were killed because the killer could get to them. It was as simple as that. They weren't guarded as well as the others. Of course this still didn't answer the question why someone wanted two Supreme Court judges dead.

He remembered that they spent most of the evening talking about their student days together in Washington, and about women. Callahan had given him a copy of the brief his girl-friend – what was her name? Darby – had written about the death of the two judges. Callahan had said it was an interesting theory. She didn't believe it, nor did he, but it was worth reading.

16

Verheek pulled the brief out of his briefcase now and started to read it. It was better written than most briefs, and he enjoyed it. The theory was implausible, but no one else had thought of it. It was worth considering. He would show it to Eric East.

♦

The phone went four times, the answering machine came on, but the caller left no message. The phone went again, and the same thing happened again. The third time Grantham climbed out of bed and answered the phone. It was still dark. 'Yes?'

'Is that Gray Grantham, of the *Washington Post*?'

'It is. Who's calling?'

'I can't give you my name.'

'OK. Why are you calling?'

'I saw your story yesterday about the White House and the possible next two Supreme Court judges.'

'Good. But why are you calling me so early in the morning?'

'I'm sorry. I'm in a pay phone. I'm on my way to work. I can't call from home or the office.'

'What kind of office?'

'I'm a lawyer.'

Great. Washington was home to half a million lawyers. 'Private or government?'

'I'd rather not say.'

'OK. Anyway, why did you call?'

A hesitation. 'I may know something about Rosenberg and Jensen.'

Grantham sat up straight. 'What, exactly?'

'Are you recording this?'

'No. Should I?'

'I don't know, Mr Grantham. I'd prefer it if you didn't record this. OK?'

'Whatever you want. I'm listening.'

'Can you trace this call?'

'I could. But you're at a pay phone – what difference would it make?'

'You're right. I'm just frightened. You see, I think I know who killed them.'

Now Grantham was standing. 'That's valuable information.'

'It could get me killed. Do you think they're following me?'

'Who? Don't worry. Tell me your name.'

'You can call me Garcia.'

'That's not your real name, is it?

'Of course not, but it's the best I can do.'

'OK, Garcia, talk to me.'

'I'm not certain, you understand. But I think I accidentally saw something at the office that I was not supposed to see.'

'Do you have a copy of it?'

'Maybe.'

'Do you want to talk or not?'

'I don't know. What will you do if I tell you something?'

'First try to find out whether it's true. We won't print the names of the killers of two Supreme Court judges in a hurry, believe me.' There was a very long silence. 'Garcia, are you still there?'

'Yes. I need to think about this. I might call you later.'

'OK, if that's what you want.'

'Sorry I woke you up.'

The phone went dead. Grantham pushed seven numbers on his phone, waited, and then pushed six more. Another wait, and then four more. The small screen on his phone showed him a row of numbers. He wrote them down on a piece of paper. The pay phone was on Fifteenth Street.

◆

East and K. O. Lewis, Voyles's second-in-command, met with Coal alone, because the President was out of Washington. They had two bits of information for him. First, they told him that cameras at the airport in Paris had recorded the arrival from Dulles of the killer Khamel.

Coal thought about this for a minute. 'What if Khamel was involved in the killings? What does it mean?'

'It means we'll never find him,' Lewis replied. 'Nine countries around the world have failed to find him for the last twenty years. It means that he was paid a lot of money by someone or some people here to do the killings.'

'So we know or we think that Khamel did the killings, but it doesn't really help us, does it?'

'No, you're right.'

'OK. What else have you got for me?'

Lewis looked at East. 'There's no real progress to report, except . . .'

'Except what?'

'Well, there's this theory which has appeared in the last twenty-four hours. A law student in New Orleans wrote it up as a brief. We call it the Pelican Brief. Here's a copy of it. Voyles liked it, but he was afraid it could hurt the President.'

'How?'

'Read it. You'll see.'

◆

This time Garcia called Grantham during office hours. He didn't tell him anything new. He was still frightened and uncertain.

19

They agreed that he would call again at lunch-time the next day. The call came from a pay phone on Pennsylvania Avenue.

◆

Later, when the President returned, Coal told him about the brief. 'The theory is implausible,' he said. 'But Voyles likes it. He probably doesn't believe the theory any more than anyone else, but we've made him look bad over these killings so far and he wants revenge. He's going to investigate this new suspect. If the press get to hear about the investigation, that could be bad for you. We'd better do something about it.'

'Is the suspect someone we know?'

'Yes.' Coal explained what was in the brief.

'Did we get a lot of money from him?'

'Millions, one way or another,' said Coal. But the President preferred not to know the various ways in which money came in, especially when they weren't always perfectly legal.

Chapter 6   Hunted!

Thomas was drinking too much over dinner. She didn't like it, and she told him so. He wanted to prove that she was wrong, so he drank even more. They had an argument.

After dinner, outside the restaurant, he pulled the keys to his Porsche out of his pocket.

'Thomas, no! You're too drunk to drive. Give me the keys.'

He held on to the keys and set off in the direction of the car park. He couldn't walk straight and his foot kept slipping off the pavement into the road. She followed him, but stayed some way behind; she was too angry, and just wanted to get back to her apartment alone. He shouted something over his shoulder about how he could drive better when he was drunk.

She stood with her arms crossed on the other side of the car park and watched him put the key into the lock. It took him three or four attempts. Then he was inside and she lost sight of him between two other cars. She heard him start the engine, though.

The explosion knocked her to the ground. She lay there for a moment, and then jumped to her feet. The Porsche was a ball of fire.

Darby ran towards it, screaming his name. Bits of the car were still falling all around her, and the heat stopped her thirty feet away. She screamed with her hands over her mouth.

A second explosion tore through the car and pushed her back. She fell and her head hit the side of a parked car hard. Everything went blank for a minute.

Then there were people everywhere, and voices shouting: 'Whose car is it? Call 911! Was there anyone in it?'

She was repeating the name Thomas. Someone put a cold cloth on her head. She heard the sound of the police and firemen coming, and then there were red and blue lights everywhere.

A black man was bending over her. 'Are you all right, miss?' he asked.

'Thomas,' she said. 'Where's Thomas?'

'Miss, who's Thomas?' asked the man. 'Was he in that car?'

She nodded and then closed her eyes. She could hear men shouting in the distance. They were all over by the burning car. She sat up and was sick between her legs. Then she felt better.

*She got up and walked away. She knew who
the bomb had been for: her. And she knew why.*

She got up and walked away. She knew who the bomb had been for: her. And she knew why.

She had to hide; they were hunting her. Were they behind her even now? She wandered deep into the French Quarter, found a cheap hotel and paid for a room with her card. As soon as she was in the room, she locked the door and curled up on the bed with all the lights on.

♦

Mrs Verheek answered the bedside phone. 'It's for you, Gavin,' she called into the bathroom, where he was shaving.

He came and took the phone from her. 'Hello,' he said angrily. Who could be calling this early in the morning?

'This is Darby Shaw. Do you know the name?'

'Yes. We share a friend.'

'Did you read the little theory I wrote?'

'Yes, the Pelican Brief, as we call it.'

'And who is "we"?'

Verheek sat up straight. She was not calling for a friendly chat. 'Why are you calling, Darby?'

'I need some answers, Mr Verheek. I'm frightened to death.'

'It's Gavin, OK?'

'OK, Gavin. Where's the brief?'

'Why? What's wrong?'

'I'll tell you in a minute. Just tell me what you did with the brief.'

'Well, I read it, and then I passed it on to someone else, who passed it on to Denton Voyles, who liked it.'

'Has anyone outside the FBI seen it?'

'I can't answer that.'

'Then I won't tell you what's happened to Thomas.'

'All right. Yes, it's been outside the FBI, but I don't know exactly where and I don't know how many people have read it.'

'He's dead, Gavin. He was murdered last night. Someone put a bomb in the car. I was lucky.'

Gavin was shocked. 'Where are you? Are you safe?'

'New Orleans. Who knows if I'm safe? They must be after me too. It was me they really wanted.'

'I'll have some men come and get you, Darby. You can't stay on the streets. Then I'll catch a plane and I'll be there by midday.'

'I don't think so. Thomas is dead because he talked to you. Why should I want to talk to you? Give me your number at work. I may call you later.'

'OK. But Darby, just tell me: did he feel any pain?'

There were tears in her voice. 'No, it was very quick.' Then she put the phone down. She could let herself cry now, because there wouldn't be time later. Crying could get her killed.

Chapter 7   Keep Moving

It was nearly time for the President's daily meeting with Voyles. By now he was tired of the whole business; he just wanted to get his men into the Supreme Court. Coal was telling him something, but he wasn't really listening. Voyles and Coal hated each other so much now that Coal had to leave the office whenever Voyles came. They had nearly fought last time. It didn't matter to Coal whether he was in or out of the office; there were enough hidden microphones and cameras for him to listen and watch any conversation there.

The President felt better knowing that Coal was at least watching. He greeted Voyles warmly at the door and led him over to the sofa for a friendly chat. Voyles was not impressed.

'Denton,' the President said, 'I want to apologize for Coal's behaviour last time.'

'He can be stupid, can't he?' Voyles said, knowing that Coal was listening.

'Yes. He's very clever, and works amazingly hard, but he goes too far sometimes. Anyway, that's all behind us now. I want you to tell me all about this Pelican Brief. How seriously are you taking it?'

Voyles tried not to smile. This was great – he had managed to get Coal and the President worried. 'We are investigating all suspects, Mr President,' he replied. 'We have fourteen men on this one.'

'I don't have to tell you, Denton,' the President continued, 'how much damage this theory could do if the press heard about it.'

'We won't tell the press, Mr President.'

'I know. All I'm saying is that I want you to pull back from this one. The theory is crazy anyway, and I could really get hurt. Do you understand what I'm saying?'

'Are you asking me not to investigate a suspect, Mr President?'

'I'm just saying that you must have better things to do with your men. The press is watching this investigation closely. You know how they are – they don't like me at all. So why don't you leave this one alone and chase the real suspects?'

'Is that what you're asking me to do?'

'I'm not asking you, Denton; I'm telling you to leave it alone for a couple of weeks. If you need to go back to it later, of course you must. But I'm still the boss around here, remember?'

◆

Gavin stayed near Voyles's office until the secretary let him in. He couldn't believe it when Voyles and Lewis told him that they were no longer investigating the Pelican theory.

'My best friend is dead because of that brief,' he said. 'He was killed by a car bomb. Someone is worried about the brief, don't you think?'

'The brief has already been very valuable to us, Gavin,' Lewis said.

'Yeah, it let you play some games with the White House,' Gavin said bitterly. 'But there's a girl out there running for her life. What am I going to tell her?'

◆

Darby made sure she could not be followed in the crowds in the shopping district. She bought some new clothes and hid her hair under a hat. She went into the Sheraton Hotel and found a row of pay phones. First she called Mrs Chen, who lived in the apartment next to hers: no, she had not seen anything; yes, there had been a knock at her door early this morning. Then she called Gavin.

'Where are you?' he asked.

'Let me explain something. For now, I'm not going to tell you or anyone else where I am. Clear?'

'Yes, but don't go home.'

'I'm not a fool. They've already been there. What did Mr Voyles say?'

'I haven't been able to see him.'

'You've been at the office for four hours, Gavin. I expected you to do better.'

'Be patient, Darby.'

'Patience will get me killed. I've got to keep moving.'

She saw a face. He walked among the tourists at the hotel's front desk. He was trying to look as though he belonged here, but his eyes were searching. The face was long and thin, and he wore round glasses. He was a little over six feet tall.

'Gavin, listen to me,' she said. 'I have to go. I can see a man I've seen before, about an hour ago.'

'OK. Take care, Darby, and call me again soon.'

'I'll try.'

Chapter 8   Photos and Phone Calls

The photographer's name was Croft. He was parked on Pennsylvania Avenue in Grantham's Volvo, because it had a phone. The pay phone was easy to see, about fifty yards in front of the car. With his powerful camera he could almost read the names in the phone book. A large woman was using the phone at the moment.

At 12:20 the woman put the phone down and walked away. From nowhere a young man in a suit appeared and walked over to the phone. Croft felt sure that this was the man. He picked up his camera and looked through it. The man was pushing numbers on the phone and looked nervous. He kept looking this way and that. Croft took a couple of pictures.

The phone in the car went three times. Croft didn't pick it up. It was Grantham at the office, signalling that this was their man. Croft used a whole film on the first camera. When the man had finished talking on the phone, he walked straight towards the Volvo along the pavement. Beautiful. Croft took several more pictures with a second camera and stopped well before the man could possibly see inside the car. An easy job.

♦

Grantham got plenty of excellent pictures from Croft. Garcia didn't look Spanish, despite the name he had chosen. He looked like thousands of other young lawyers up and down the country.

From Garcia he got nothing. It didn't matter. He let him talk about his wife and child, and how frightened he was. One day, and one day soon, Garcia would give him the information, whatever it was.

From Sarge he got a copy of a White House document naming Khamel as the probable killer of Rosenberg and Jensen. This was good. There was little in the office files about Khamel, and only two pictures, which looked like two different people, but he wrote it up into a story and they decided to use both pictures and the story on the front page the next day.

♦

The phone was going. After twenty-four hours on the run, she had drunk a bottle of wine the night before and fallen asleep on her bed in the Marriott Hotel. But first she had cut off her long red hair and coloured it black; they would be expecting blonde. They would also be expecting her to run away, so despite her fears she stayed in New Orleans. They would be watching all the police stations, so she had stayed away from them.

The phone was still going. She picked it up and heard 'Darby? This is Gavin.'

Now she was awake. 'How did you find me?'

'We are the FBI. We have our ways.'

'Wait. Let me think. Of course, you can trace me when I use my cards to pay for things. How stupid of me! But if you can find me, they can find me too. They could be outside the door now.'

'Stay in small hotels, then, and pay with cash. Now, listen. I'm coming to New Orleans; it's Thomas's funeral tomorrow.

I think we should meet tonight. You have to trust me, Darby.'

'What did Voyles say?'

Gavin hesitated. 'We're taking no action at this time.'

'That's lawyer talk, Gavin. What does it mean?'

'I don't want to talk on the phone. That's why we have to meet.'

'No. Tell me why Voyles is doing nothing about this.'

'I'm not sure why. Honestly.'

'What do you think, Gavin? Do you think Thomas was killed because of the brief?'

'Yes.'

'Thanks. If Thomas was murdered because of the brief, then we know who killed him. And if we know who killed Thomas, then we know who killed Rosenberg and Jensen. Am I right?'

'Probably.'

'That's good enough – "probably" means "yes" when a lawyer says it. But the FBI is still doing nothing about my suspect.'

'Calm down, Darby. Let's meet tonight and talk about this. I could save your life.'

She carefully put the receiver of the phone under the pillow. She threw her things into a bag and left the room. She walked up two floors to the seventeenth, then took the lift down to the tenth. Then she walked down the stairs to the ground floor. She hid in the women's room for half an hour, and then left the hotel.

On Dumaine Street, in the French Quarter, she found an empty cafe with a phone at the back. She called Verheek.

'Where will you stay tonight?' she asked him.

'At the Hilton.'

'I'll call late tonight or early in the morning.'

29

'Can you get the *Washington Post* down there? You should read it today.'

'I can't wait. I'll speak to you later.'

She bought a *Post* and read it at another café. If the report was right, it fitted in with her theory. The local paper had a picture of Thomas on the second page, with a long story about the explosion. The police were looking for a white female whom several witnesses had seen there at the time. She looked slowly at the photo of Thomas. He was so handsome. Tears filled her eyes.

◆

Alice Stark, Darby's best friend, got the key to the apartment from Mrs Chen and let herself in. She had been there plenty of times before, and everything looked all right. Nothing was out of place; the whole apartment was tidy. The kitchen smelled of stale food.

It was dark when she got there, but Darby had told her not to switch on the lights, and certainly not to open the curtains. She used a torch to see her way around.

She sat down at the computer and turned it on. She looked for the files Darby had mentioned, but they weren't there. By the light of the torch she looked in the boxes of diskettes; they were empty.

Alice returned the key to Mrs Chen and walked half a mile to where she had left her car. She met Darby as arranged in the restaurant, and she told her what she had discovered. Darby did not seem surprised, and refused to answer Alice's questions.

◆

Verheek was angry. She had said she would call him. Now it was midnight and she still hadn't called. He could save her life if she called. He had to do something. He decided to visit a few student bars to find out if anyone knew her and had seen her recently. He got back to his room at three in the morning. There were no messages. She hadn't called. Was she still alive?

Chapter 9   Searching for Darby

Another phone call from Garcia. The man still wouldn't talk. Why was he calling him before dawn on a Saturday? They'd had the same conversation every time – that he had to think about the safety of his wife and child, that he had seen something in his office – but there was never anything new.

Grantham had just gone back to sleep when the phone went again.

'Hello?' It was not Garcia this time; it was a female voice. 'Is this Gray Grantham of the *Washington Post*?' He must get an unlisted telephone number.

'It is. And who are you?'

'Are you still on the story about Rosenberg and Jensen?'

'Yes.'

'Have you heard of the Pelican Brief?'

'The Pelican Brief. No. What is it?'

'It contains a theory about who killed the judges. It was given to the FBI last Monday by a man called Thomas Callahan. Suddenly, on Wednesday, Callahan is killed by a car bomb.'

'How do you know all this?'

'I wrote the brief.'

He was wide awake now, listening hard. 'Where are you?'

31

'New Orleans.'

'Are you in danger?'

'I think so. But I'm OK for now. I'll call you again soon. See if you can find out anything about the brief.'

◆

She came early to Thomas's funeral, and she would stay late. She found an empty room on the third floor of a student building that looked out over the university church. She sat with her face to the window and saw his parents and brother arrive. Students and staff came in twos and threes. She pressed a handkerchief to her eyes.

Then she saw him: it was the thin-faced man with glasses! He was wearing a coat and tie. He walked towards the church, looking carefully in every direction. First they kill him, then they come to his funeral.

Ten minutes later he came back out of the church. He looked sad, as if Thomas had been a friend. He put a cigarette in his mouth and walked past some parked cars and behind the church. Two minutes later, another man got out of one of the cars and followed him. The two of them reappeared after a minute, walking together now. Then Thin-face disappeared down the street while the other man, who was short, returned to his car and waited for the funeral service to finish.

◆

The Cubans lowered the small rubber boat into the water from their ship. They heard the sound of the little engine as the man went west through the darkness towards the coast.

He would never use a commercial airline again; the photographs in Paris were embarrassing for a professional like himself, and his client was not pleased. Now he was going to have to do two jobs in a single month, which he had never done before. But this one would be easy – just a young woman.

In the hotel room in New Orleans, he spoke on the phone to a man calling himself Mr Sneller.

'Tell me about her,' he said.

'There are two photos in the briefcase.'

Khamel opened the case and took out the photos. 'I've got them. She's beautiful. It will almost be a pity to kill her.'

'Yes. But all that red hair has gone. We found some hair on the floor of a hotel room. She has coloured it black.'

'Where is she now?'

'We don't know. She has stopped using her cards to pay for things. She took out a lot of money from her bank, and since then she has disappeared. We think she's still in New Orleans, though. Someone was in her apartment last night. We just missed them. The bomb failed. We don't expect you to fail.'

◆

Gavin was tired. He had spent two nights searching the bars, and he was too old for these late nights. When the phone went, he was still asleep.

'Gavin?'

'Darby, is that you?'

'Yes.'

'Why haven't you called before?'

'That doesn't matter now. You should know that they're here, in New Orleans. I've seen two of them – a thin-faced man and a short man. They were at the funeral service yesterday.'

'Where were you?'

The phone went dead. Gavin picked it up and threw it across his hotel room.

'Watching. How long will you be in town?'

'Until we meet. When will that be?'

'I don't know yet. I'll call again soon.'

The phone went dead. Gavin picked it up and threw it across his hotel room.

Chapter 10   Another Body

The first thing she did when she woke up on Sunday morning was listen. Was the door opening? Was the floor outside making a noise? When she was sure she was safe, she thought about Thomas. She remembered their times together; she remembered how he loved her. It was a surprise for him, the first time he had really been in love. And she loved him too.

After a few minutes of thinking about Thomas, she thought about *them*. She had to think like them too, to stay alive. Where would they be today? Where could she go? Was it time to move hotels again? Yes. Did they know that she was now a blonde?

She felt hungry. She had hardly eaten for days. This hotel didn't do breakfast on Sundays, so she had to go out. She left by the back door, through the kitchen.

He saw her when she reached Burgundy Street. The hair was different, but she couldn't change her long legs. He started to follow her.

◆

Khamel was practising his English when the phone went. It was Sneller. 'She's here,' he said. 'One of our men saw her this morning. He chased her, but she noticed him and lost him in the football crowds.'

Khamel said, 'So how am I supposed to find her, if your men can't tell me where she's staying?'

'It might not matter,' Sneller said. 'There's an FBI lawyer in town. The fool has been visiting bars and asking questions about her, spreading his name around. He's asked anyone who knows her to contact him at his hotel, the Hilton. My men will continue trying to find the girl, and you can stay close to him. He's in Room 1909. He was Callahan's best friend. She might call him.'

◆

Gavin was lying on his bed, watching TV. It was eleven at night. He would wait until twelve and then try to sleep. He had decided to go home tomorrow if she didn't call. He couldn't find her. It wasn't his fault: even taxi-drivers got lost in this city.

When the phone went, he switched the TV off and picked it up.

'It's me, Gavin,' she said.

'You're alive,' he said.

'Yes, but I was followed today. It was the short man.'

'Did he follow you from somewhere?'

'No, he just happened to see me in the streets.'

'Listen, Darby, I can't wait here any more. I've got a job to go back to. I want to leave New Orleans tomorrow, and I want you to come with me. I'll have three men guarding you, and you'll be safe. You can tell us all you know, and then the FBI will finish the job.'

Darby thought for a minute. 'All right. Behind your hotel there's a shopping area called Riverwalk.'

'I know it.'

'Good. Find a shop called Frenchmen's Bend and be there, at the back of the shop, at midday tomorrow. I don't know what you look like, so wear a black shirt and carry a newspaper.'

'This is silly.'

'No, it's not. I've had to learn fast how to stay alive. Believe me, this is the way to do it.'

'OK, you're the boss.'

'That's right. Only you and I will leave the city. I don't want anyone else knowing about this. Do you understand?'

'All right.'

'How tall are you?'

'About five feet, ten inches.'

'And how much to you weigh?'

'About a hundred kilos. I usually lie about it. I'm going to start doing some exercise.'

'I'll see you tomorrow, Gavin.'

'I hope so.'

He put the phone down and smiled. 'Great! At last!' he said out loud. He went into the bathroom for a shower.

When he came out, the room was dark. Dark? But he had left the light on, hadn't he? He started to walk over to the light switch.

The first blow caught him in the throat. He fell to his knees, which made the second blow easy. It landed like a rock on the back of his neck, and Gavin was dead.

Khamel switched on a light. He lifted up the body and put it on the bed. He turned the sound on the television up loud, opened his bag and took out a cheap gun. He held it to the right side of Gavin's head and fired. Then he carefully put the gun in Gavin's right hand and curled the fingers around it. It wouldn't take a doctor very long to find out how Gavin had really died, but Khamel didn't need very long – by the evening of the next day he would be out of the country.

He opened up the receiver of the telephone and took out the little microphone. He pulled the recorder out from under the bed. Finally, he checked that the cupboard where he had waited was clean. Then he left the room. No one had seen him enter, and no one saw him leave.

Chapter 11   Riverwalk

Grantham couldn't find out anything about the brief. Even Sarge hadn't heard of it. When Darby's call came through to his office on Monday morning he had nothing to tell her.

'It doesn't matter. I'll tell you everything soon, I think. I don't want to die without telling the world what I know. They're following me here in New Orleans.'

'Who?'

'The same people who killed Rosenberg and Jensen. If you've read the report about Callahan's death, you know about the white female the police want to talk to. That's me. My name is Darby Shaw. Thomas Callahan was my teacher and my lover. I wrote the brief, gave it to him, he passed it on to the FBI, who took it to the White House, and you know what happened next. Are you recording this?'

'I'm writing it down,' Grantham said.

'I'm going to leave New Orleans. I'll call you from somewhere else tomorrow. Can you get a copy of the list of people who gave large amounts of money to help the President get elected?'

'Easy; it's public information. I'll have it by the time you call. Do you have a copy of the brief?'

'No, but I remember it all.'

'And you know who's doing the killing?'

'Yes, and as soon as I tell you, your life will be in danger too.'

'Tell me now.'

'Not so fast. I'll call you tomorrow.'

After the phone conversation Grantham went in to see his boss, Smith Keen. He explained the situation to him. Keen was excited, but said, 'Even if she tells us what's in the brief, we can't print the story; we'll need an independent witness.'

'I'm working on it,' Grantham said, and told him about Garcia.

'This is going to be big,' Keen said. 'This is going to put the *Post* right back up at the top.'

♦

She arrived on Riverwalk at eleven. She sat in a restaurant and nervously drank a coffee while watching the people pass. She didn't see Thin-face or Shorty or anyone else she recognized. At 11:45 she got up and walked towards Frenchmen's Bend. If he wasn't there by 12:15 she would leave. But he was there, wearing the black shirt and carrying a newspaper. He looked nervous too. She liked that. At exactly twelve o'clock he walked into the shop and went to the back.

She came up behind him and said, 'Gavin.'

He had practised Gavin's voice for hours, but wasn't sure he had it exactly right. He turned around quickly and said, 'Darby.' Then he pretended to cough. She wouldn't expect the same voice from someone with a cold. 'Let's get out of here,' he said.

'Follow me,' she said. Darby took his hand and led him out of the shop and towards the river.

'Have you seen them?' he asked.

'No, but they're around somewhere.'

'Where are we going?'

'Just come with me.'

'You're walking too fast, Darby. It will look strange to people. Let me make a phone call. I can have men here in ten minutes and then we'll be safe.' He was pleased with himself; he sounded just right.

'No,' she said, but she slowed down. They joined the queue for the riverboat *Bayou Queen*. 'The boat will take us to where I've parked a car,' she explained. 'Then we get out of here fast.'

Khamel was uncomfortable; he was wearing a great many underclothes, so that he would look as fat as Verheek. But he could wait an hour until they were out of the city. And then . . .

The man with the gun pushed his way through the queue. He had killed before, but never in such a public place. The queue was moving, but he was getting through it. The man and the woman were just about to step on to the boat when he reached them. He pulled the gun out of his pocket, held it to the man's head and fired. He disappeared through the crowd.

Gavin was falling to the ground. Darby screamed and moved back in horror. 'He's got a gun!' a woman shouted, and pointed at Gavin, who was on his hands and knees, with a small gun in his right hand. Blood poured from his nose and chin, and formed a small pool under his face. His head was hanging down until it nearly touched the ground. He was speaking some words in a language Darby didn't recognize.

'He's Egyptian,' someone in the crowd said.

He fell forward, dropping the gun into the water, and died in a widening pool of blood. Darby walked away as the crowd moved forwards to see the dead man, and two policemen started to push their way through.

◆

40

The man with the gun pushed his way through the queue.
He had killed before, but never in such a public place.

She left Riverwalk after dark. She had bought new clothes and wore a new coat as well. She waved at a taxi.

'How much to take me to Baton Rouge?' she asked.

'That's a long way,' the driver said. 'You should go by bus or train.'

'How much?' she asked again.

'One hundred and fifty dollars,' the man said, after a moment's thought.

'Here's two hundred,' she said. 'Get me there fast.' Thomas had talked to her about his friend Gavin Verheek. She knew he wasn't an Egyptian.

Chapter 12   Darby Explains

Voyles sent East down to New Orleans to learn the truth about Verheek's death. Lewis brought the news to his office.

'Denton, when are we going to start taking this Pelican Brief seriously?' he asked. 'People keep dying because of it. We'd better investigate it. It must be Mattiece.'

'I know,' Voyles said. 'We'll send down a team of men, but I don't want the fool in the White House or Coal to hear that we're investigating it – I want to surprise them. When the President told me to leave the brief alone, I was carrying a small recorder in my pocket. I've got every word, loud and clear. If we find that the brief is accurate, the press will love us, and we can let them know that the President told us not to investigate it.'

'That'll be the end of him and Coal,' Lewis said happily.

'I know. He'll have no chance in the election next year. We've got him.'

They smiled at each other. 'But what about Mattiece?' Lewis

said. 'If he hadn't killed all those people, we wouldn't have thought the brief was right. He must be crazy.'

'There are rumours that he is,' Voyles replied. 'I've spoken to the CIA. They had men in New Orleans. They don't know where Mattiece is. He's probably not in this country. He owns houses all over the world. We'll need their help to get him. They were following the girl too, but they lost her in Chicago airport. She could be anywhere by now.'

'She could be dead,' Lewis said. 'Mattiece's men are following her as well.'

◆

Grantham traced two old photographs of her – one from her high school, one from her first university. He pinned them up beside his desk. She was beautiful.

She called him as she had promised. He had read about the killing of a lawyer in New Orleans, and she told him the true story. She also told him about the other killing, which had not appeared in the newspapers. Then she said, 'Can you come to New York tomorrow, Grantham?'

'Of course. It'll only take a few hours. But please call me Gray.' He looked at the photographs of her.

'I'll ring tomorrow morning to tell you where to meet me. And tomorrow I'll tell you who killed Rosenberg and Jensen.'

'Do you know who did it?'

'I know who paid for the killings. I know his name. I know his business and his politics.'

'And you'll tell me tomorrow.'

'If I'm still alive.'

A pause. 'Perhaps we should talk immediately,' he said.

◆

They met in her room in the St Moritz Hotel in New York. They chatted for a while, getting to know each other. It was the first normal conversation Darby had had for a week, and it was a great pleasure. They sent out for some food, and after they had eaten he switched on a recorder and she told him a story:

'For centuries, the Mississippi River has been carrying mud down to the sea. Where the river meets the sea, marshes have spread out over an enormous area. These marshes are the home for a great many rare and unusual animals, birds, reptiles and fish.

'Then oil was discovered there in 1930. The oil companies began to destroy the marshes. Where the river mud had been creating new land, now the sea was able to wash the land away. Since the discovery of oil, tens of thousands of acres of Louisiana marshland has gone. Every fourteen minutes, another acre disappears under water.

'In 1979 an oil company owned by Victor Mattiece found a very rich oilfield, worth thousands of millions of dollars. Mattiece wanted it all. He knew that others would buy the surrounding land if they heard there was a major oilfield there, so he pretended that nothing had happened. He stopped work there, and waited. Slowly and patiently, as the years passed, he bought the surrounding land. He created new companies, lots of them, so that no one would know that he was the buyer. At last he was ready to begin drilling.

'Then a small environmental group called Green Rescue made a legal request to the courts to stop the drilling. The request was unexpected, because for so long Louisiana had profited from the oil companies. The court in Lafayette agreed that all drilling should stop until the case was settled.

'Mattiece knew that this could take years. He was dangerously angry. He spent weeks with his lawyers, making plans. But every move they made was disallowed by the courts.

'People were sympathetic to Green Rescue's case. A lot of wildlife was at risk. The marshland where Mattiece wanted to drill was home to a great many rare and beautiful sea birds, including brown pelicans. There were very few of these pelicans left. When people thought about the case, they thought about the pelicans.

'At last the case came to trial. Green Rescue lost, and that was not surprising: Mattiece had spent millions of dollars and had the best lawyers in the country. But the judge still forbade the drilling to start. The pelican was a protected bird under Louisiana law, and Green Rescue weren't finished yet: they would take the case all the way to the Supreme Court.'

'How long would it take to reach the Supreme Court?' Gray asked.

'Between three and five years.'

'By then Rosenberg would be dead anyway.'

'Yes, but it might be a Democratic President who was choosing the judge to take his place; Mattiece couldn't take that chance. And Jensen was always soft on environmental cases. Mattiece needed two Republican judges in there, both of whom were supporters of big business.'

'Can you prove that all the companies involved in buying the land in Louisiana are owned by Mattiece?'

'It's in the brief, and I've written it all out for you. And then there's the photograph.'

'Tell me.'

'Seven years ago, before the President was elected, he was in New Orleans getting money for the Republicans. Although Mattiece stays out of the public eye, he was there that day, and some clever photographer got a picture of him shaking hands with the President. Both of them are smiling, and they look like old friends. It's beautiful.'

'I can easily find a copy of that. This whole thing is beautiful. It's the biggest story since Watergate★ – maybe even bigger.' Gray turned off the recorder and sat back in his chair. They were silent for a short while. Then he asked, 'Do you think Mattiece himself chose Rosenberg and Jensen?'

'No, I'm sure he had advice from a lawyer. He's got lawyers all over the country.'

Gray sat up again. 'Does he have any in Washington?'

'Yes, there are two firms there who do some work for him – Brim, Stearns and Kidlow is one of them; the other is White and Blazevich, a very old, Republican firm. But why are you interested?'

Gray quickly told her about Garcia. 'Maybe he works at one of those two firms,' he said. 'That would make it much easier to find him.'

They were both tired. She asked him to sleep on the sofa in her room that night, so that she could get a good night's sleep for the first time for days. He agreed. She was so beautiful that he would do anything to be close her; he would even sleep on a five-foot sofa.

Chapter 13   Washington

Darby worked in the library all morning and rang Grantham at midday. She had been reading lists of the members at both the

★ Watergate is the name of an office building in Washington in which members of President Nixon's Government in the early 1970s put hidden microphones. This was the first of many crimes that people in Nixon's government had committed, and they were discovered by two newspaper reporters. The stories the reporters wrote helped to bring the Government down.

Washington law firms that worked for Mattiece; there was no one called Garcia on either list, of course. There were four Spanish names among the 190 lawyers who worked for Brim, Stearns and Kidlow, but none among the 412 who worked for White and Blazevich.

She rang Gray with this information from a pay phone in a café on Sixth Avenue. As she turned to leave she saw the short man who had been looking for her in New Orleans. He was here, in New York, walking the streets. He didn't look inside the café, however. For the moment she was safe, but it was time to leave New York. Two hours later, she was at Newark airport.

When this was all over – if she was still alive – where could she go? She thought of the thousands of islands in the Caribbean; no one could find her there. She no longer wanted to practise law. All she wanted to do was reach her twenty-fifth birthday, and maybe her thirtieth too.

◆

Croft spent a week waiting outside the offices of Brim, Stearns and Kidlow. There were plenty of lawyers who looked as young as Garcia, and they all dressed similarly in dark suits, but there was no Garcia. He was sure of it.

◆

Some of the people employed by the White House didn't work at the White House; some were so secret that their offices were elsewhere and very few people knew of their existence. Matthew Barr was one of these shadowy people.

He was riding in the back of the car with Coal. Coal was silent while Barr read the Pelican Brief. When he had finished, Barr said, 'I'd love to know how much of this is true.'

'So would we,' Coal said.

'What did the President say about it?'

'He agreed that the theory was implausible, so he asked Voyles not to investigate it.'

'Really? And what if it's true?'

'Then the President has got problems. Me too.'

They rode in silence for a while and watched the traffic. Then Coal said, 'We need to know if the brief is true.'

'If people are dying, it's true. Why else did Callahan and Verheek die?'

There was no other reason, and Coal knew it. 'I want you to do something.'

'Find the girl?'

'No, go to Mattiece and talk to him.'

'It won't be easy. He isn't exactly listed in the phone book.'

'You can do it. You've done more difficult things for us in the past. You've done worse for us too.'

'And you think Victor will trust me and tell me his secrets?'

'Why not? You're not a policeman. You can help him; you can tell him that the press will have the story soon and so it would be a good idea for him to disappear. Then he'll trust you.'

'What if it's true? What will you do next?'

'The first thing will be for the President to appoint two nature-lovers to the Supreme Court; that will show people that we really care for the environment. Then, at the same time, he will get the FBI to start an official investigation into Victor Mattiece.'

Barr was smiling with admiration. 'What about the photograph?' he asked.

'Easy. It's seven years old. We say that in those days Mattiece was a good citizen, not a madman as he is now. Anyway, by Sunday I'll tell you where he is. I've got a man working on it. Be ready to leave.'

◆

Darby called Gray at 9:30 the next morning at his office. 'I'm here,' she said.

'Where are you calling from?' Gray asked.

'I'm staying at the Tabard Inn. I saw an old friend in New York and decided it was time to leave. I hope I didn't bring any of them with me. I bought two plane tickets with my card, for them to follow, but I paid cash for the one I really used. Even then I changed planes four times. If they follow me here, they must be magicians. If I see any of them here, I think I'll just surrender.'

'When do we meet?'

'Meet me in the restaurant here at nine tonight. But, Gray, don't use your own car; hire another one. And be ready to stay away from your home and office for a few days. I've booked you a room at the Marbury Hotel.'

'Surely the office is safe, Darby.'

'I'm not in the mood to argue. If you're going to be difficult, Gray, I'll simply disappear. I'm sure I'll live longer out of the country, anyway. I've got to go now. You be careful.'

◆

The Marbury was close to where his boss, Smith Keen, lived, and there were some things they had to talk about. The next morning he rang Keen from his room and they arranged to meet outside the front of the hotel in fifteen minutes. While they drove around in Keen's car they discussed various ways in which they could use the information they had. They agreed that finding Garcia was the key to the whole story; without Garcia they had little more than rumour and an unlikely theory. They hoped that Garcia's information really was as important as they were guessing it was.

She had told him to stay off the streets and to eat in his room. After Keen had left him near his hotel, he bought a sandwich and a cup of coffee, and returned to his room. An Asian cleaning woman was working outside his room.

'Did you forget something, sir?' she asked.

Gray looked at her. 'What do you mean?'

'You just left your room, sir, and now you're back.'

'I left two hours ago.'

'No, sir. A man left your room ten minutes ago.' She hesitated and looked at his face closely. 'But now I see that it was another man, sir.'

He walked quickly to the stairs and ran all the way down to the ground floor. What was in his room? Nothing important – just some clothes. Nothing about Darby. Her phone number at the Tabard Inn was in his pocket.

He had to find her, and quick.

Chapter 14   Curtis D. Morgan

Darby spent the day in the Georgetown law library, reading and taking notes about the members of the Washington law firms that Mattiece used. It was boring work, and her mind often wandered. She thought a lot about Thomas.

◆

Matthew Barr went to New Orleans, where he met a lawyer who told him to fly to a certain hotel in Fort Lauderdale, Florida. He wouldn't tell Barr what was going to happen there, but when Barr arrived he found a room waiting for him. A note at the front desk of the hotel said he would receive a phone call in the early morning.

He called Fletcher Coal at home at ten and told him the news.

◆

She stepped on the note when she opened her door. It said: *Darby, I'm in the garden. It's urgent. Gray.* She locked the door, went downstairs, through the restaurant and out into the garden. She found him sitting at a small table, half hidden behind a wall.

'Why are you here?' she demanded in a whisper.

He told her what had happened, and what he'd done for the rest of the day. He had spent it riding round the city in a dozen different taxis, waiting for dark. Then he came to the Tabard. He was certain that no one had followed him.

She listened. She watched the restaurant and the entrance to the garden, and heard every word.

'I have no idea how anyone could find my room,' he said.

'Did you tell anyone your room number?'

He thought for a second. 'Only Smith Keen, but he didn't have time to tell anyone else.'

'Where were you when you told him?'

'In his car.'

She shook her head slowly. 'I told you not to tell anyone, didn't I? You think this is all a game. It's not, Gray, it's real. This isn't just a great newspaper story, which is going to make Gray Grantham famous and win him prizes. I've seen people die. God knows how many times I've been close to death myself. These people are dangerous, and they're professionals. They know about you and the *Washington Post*. They've probably been listening to you since you wrote the first story about this matter. They'll have microphones hidden in your apartment, your car and your office. It looks as though they've got microphones in Keen's car as well. Do you understand what I'm saying? Last night at dinner we tried to pretend we were two normal people getting to know each other. But that wasn't real: this is real.'

She was right, of course. He felt like a schoolchild in front of an angry teacher.

'You can stay here tonight,' she said, 'and tomorrow I'll find you another small hotel.'

◆

After breakfast the next morning she got on the phone. She rang the Georgetown law school and pretended to be from White and Blazevich. She said that their computers were not working, and that for the sake of her records she needed to know which students had worked for White and Blazevich last summer. She waited, with her hand over the mouthpiece of the phone, and looked at Gray. The secretary from the law school came back on the phone. 'Seven of them,' Darby said. 'Thank you.' She wrote down their names. 'And do you have their addresses, please? We need them for our records.' She wrote down this information too.

'That was brilliant,' Gray said when she had finished.

'Now all we need to do is find as many of these students as we can, show them your photograph of Garcia, and hope that one of them recognizes him and can tell us his real name.'

'Why couldn't we just wait outside the firm's building until he came out, and then follow him? That's what Croft was doing at Brim, Stearns and Kidlow.'

'Too risky. It seems likely that White and Blazevich were involved in some way in the killings. There are people who know my face, and we know they're looking for you too. What if they're guarding White and Blazevich? They would see us, and then we'd be dead.'

They hired a car and began to try to find the seven students. Gray found two of them at home and Darby spoke to another as he was leaving a class at the school; none of them recognized Garcia. They met at 10:45 and compared notes. At eleven, students were leaving their classes and she found another of the seven students, but he too knew nothing. A fifth was working in the library; she didn't like answering Darby's questions, but she admitted that she didn't know Garcia.

Only two left – Edward Linney and Judith Wilson. Wilson was expected back at her apartment at one o'clock, so Gray spent the rest of the morning trying to find Linney, but he was not at home and no one at the school seemed to know where he was. They hadn't seen him for several weeks.

They drove together to Judith Wilson's apartment. She wasn't there at one, so they waited. She arrived an hour later. Gray jumped out of the car, ran up to her and caught her at her front door. He showed her the photograph, and Darby saw her shake her head.

'Linney had better be good,' he said as he got back into the car. 'But where is he?'

'I hope we find him today,' she said, 'because tomorrow I leave the country if we don't.'

Back at the law school, one of his fellow students at last told them where he was: in a private hospital. He was well on the way to becoming an alcoholic, and his parents had ordered him to spend some time there. The nurse at the front desk of the hospital told Gray that Mr Linney was in Room 22, but refused to let him see him. Gray asked to see the manager, and while the nurse was fetching him Gray whispered to Darby, 'Room 22.'

She left the waiting-room and boldly walked to his room. She knocked and went in. The young man looked surprised to see her.

'I'm Sara Jacobs,' she said. 'I work for the *Washington Post*. May I ask you a question?'

'Yes, but how did you get in?'

'I just walked in. You worked at White and Blazevich last summer, didn't you? Do you recognize this man?' She showed him the photograph.

'Yes, he's . . . what's his name? I can't remember. He works in the oil and gas department.'

Darby held her breath.

Linney closed his eyes and thought. 'Morgan. Yes, that's it. His surname is Morgan, but I can't remember his first name. What's this all about?'

'I'll tell you later,' Darby said, and left.

Gray was waiting for her back in the car. She didn't say anything but immediately looked at the notes she had taken in the law library. There he was. 'Garcia is Curtis D. Morgan,' she said. 'Let's go.'

Chapter 15   Two Appointments

After five hours at sea in the small, fast boat, every bone in Matthew Barr's body was aching, and he was wet and cold. His only companion had been a man called Larry, who was extremely tall and looked very strong. Larry had met him in Fort Lauderdale and had not said a word to him since then.

They landed in a country Barr believed was the Bahamas. A car took them to a small airfield, where a Lear jet was waiting. The flight took about forty-five minutes. Another car took them to a large house. Barr had no idea where they were.

Barr was met by a man who called himself Emil, who led him round the outside of the house to a sun-room.

'I'm afraid you must take off your shoes,' Emil said with a polite smile, 'and be careful not to step on the towels.'

Inside, Barr saw that towels were lying on the floor of the sun-room, making paths around the room. A door on the other side of the room opened, and Victor Mattiece came in.

Barr stared. Mattiece was an extraordinary sight. He was extremely thin, and had long grey hair and a beard. He wore only

Mattiece was extremely thin, and had long grey hair and a beard.
He wore only a pair of black sports shorts.

a pair of black sports shorts. His toenails were yellow and very long. He looked completely crazy.

'Sit over there,' he said, pointing at a chair. 'Don't step on the towels.'

When Barr was seated, Mattiece asked, 'What do you want?' He was staring out of a window.

'The President sent me,' Barr began.

'He did not. Fletcher Coal sent you.'

'All right. We need to know whether the Pelican Brief is true. Have you read it?'

'Have you?'

'Yes.'

'Does Mr Coal believe it to be true?'

'I don't know. He's very worried. That's why I'm here, Mr Mattiece. We have to know.'

'What if it *is* true?'

'Then we have problems.'

Mattiece turned away from the window, looked at Barr and said, 'Do you know what I think? I think Coal is the problem. He let too many people see the brief.'

Barr could not believe what he was hearing. The man who had ordered so many deaths was blaming someone else for the situation. 'Is it true, Mr Mattiece? That's all I want to know.'

Behind Barr, a door opened without a sound. Larry, in his socks and avoiding the towels, stepped silently into the room.

Mattiece walked over to the door and said softly, 'Of course it's true.' He left the sun-room and went into the garden.

Now what? Barr thought.

Larry put the rope round Barr's neck, and Barr did not hear or feel anything until it was too late. Mattiece did not want blood on the floor, so Larry simply broke his neck.

◆

They reached the building where White and Blazevich's offices were before five o'clock. She was wearing a dress, and Gray said she looked just right. She could tell that he liked the way she looked, and she found to her surprise that it didn't make her angry, just a little sad about Thomas.

She walked up to the secretary at the desk, who said, 'Can I help you?'

'Yes, I have an appointment at five o'clock with Curtis Morgan. My name is Dorothy Blythe.'

The secretary's mouth fell open and she said nothing.

Darby's heart stopped. 'Is something the matter?'

'Can you wait a moment?' the secretary said. She got up and disappeared into another room.

Run, Darby's mind was telling her, run! There's something wrong here. But before she had time to do anything, the secretary returned with a man.

'Good afternoon,' he said. 'I'm Jarreld Schwabe, one of the partners of the firm. You say you have an appointment with Curtis Morgan?'

'Yes. Is there a problem?'

'There's nothing in his appointment book.'

'Well, that's your fault, not mine.'

'And what was the meeting about?'

She felt weak. 'I don't see why I have to tell you that. Why can't I see Mr Morgan?'

'Because he's dead.'

She was in shock. 'Dead?'

'Yes,' Schwabe said. 'He was mugged in the street. I'm sorry. I can see this has been a shock for you.'

She decided to act really upset. She didn't want them to ask any more questions; she wanted them to think that she was just a weak young woman. 'I'm sorry,' she said, 'I think I'd better go. I'll phone again for another appointment.'

Schwabe led her to the lift himself.

♦

Edwin Sneller knew that he and his men had been wasting their time in New York; the place was just too big. Then at last she moved some money from her bank in New Orleans to Grantham's bank in Washington. Sneller's client owned the bank, so he received any information he asked for. That meant that she was in Washington, and that she and the reporter were working together. He had two men with him, and he had asked for more. They had to do the job quickly. But he felt less confident without Khamel. The girl had escaped so far, and she could be hiding anywhere. He would start with the *Washington Post* building: Grantham had to come back there some time.

♦

Gray found Curtis D. Morgan's address in the suburbs, and they drove out together to the house. Mrs Morgan's father, however, refused to let them in to see her. Gray left his business card, so that she could call him if she wanted to. He told her father that Morgan had spoken to him three times just before he died.

'Is that the end of Garcia?' Darby asked as they drove away.

'We'll see tomorrow,' he said. 'How do you feel at the moment? Do you feel safe? I'll be glad to sleep in your room tonight, just like I did in New York.'

'But I don't have a sofa here,' she said. 'Where would you sleep?' She was smiling and this was a good sign. But then she remembered Callahan. 'I'm not ready, Gray. I'm sorry.' She rested her head on his shoulder while he drove the car. 'I'm still frightened to death,' she said.

Chapter 16   Morgan's Story

Beverly Morgan called Gray at four o'clock the next morning. 'My father would be angry with me if he knew I was calling,' she said. 'The reporters were horrible to us after Curtis was killed. But I need to talk to someone.'

She asked him how he knew her husband, and Gray explained about his phone calls, and the murders of Rosenberg and Jensen. He spoke to her patiently for a long time, until he won her confidence.

'What do you think he knew?' she asked.

'I have no idea. If he had written something down on paper, where would it be?'

'In our lock-box in the bank. But that's where all his legal papers were, so I've already looked in there. I did find another key in his desk, though, last Saturday.'

Gray held his breath. 'A key to another lock-box?'

'Yes, a box at First Columbia Bank. That's odd, because we've never used that bank. I wasn't in a hurry to go to the bank and look in the box, because I already had all his legal papers. Maybe it was even something I wouldn't want to see.'

'Would you like me to look in the box for you?' Gray asked.

'I hoped you would say that. Yes, please.'

'I'll come round and get the key now.'

◆

He and Darby drove to the bank the next morning. Mrs Morgan had given Gray written permission to open the lock-box, so the clerk let them into the strong-room. It didn't take them long to empty the box: all it held was a thin envelope.

Darby opened the envelope when they were back in the car. Inside was a document written by Morgan and properly signed by a legal witness. The document started: 'Since you are reading this, I am probably dead.' It was a powerful first sentence.

In the document Morgan described who he was and where he worked. He said that he often worked for one of the firm's clients who was called Victor Mattiece. The partner in charge of Mr Mattiece was F. Sims Wakefield. Morgan explained the Louisiana case and how important it was to Mr Mattiece. It was important to White and Blazevich too, since Mattiece had promised them a share of the profits from the oil.

On or about 28 September, the document continued, Morgan had been in Wakefield's office collecting some files. When he returned to his own office, he found that by mistake he had picked up a note from Wakefield's desk together with the files. A copy of the note was joined on to Morgan's document. The note was dated 28 September and was from Marty Velmano, another partner. It read: *Sims: Tell our client that the Court will be easier on him if Rosenberg is retired. The second retirement is a bit unusual – it is Jensen (who, as you know, has those other problems).* The note amazed and frightened Morgan. Realizing its importance, he made a copy of it and returned the original to the bottom of the pile of files.

Ten minutes later Wakefield came into his office, looking pale and worried. They found the note under the files and Wakefield asked Morgan if he had read it; Morgan said no. Wakefield looked at him very closely, but seemed satisfied.

That night he left the papers on his desk very tidy. The next morning he could see that someone had searched his desk. He began to see Velmano in Wakefield's office more than usual. Wakefield stopped him working for Mattiece.

Then Rosenberg and Jensen were killed. He was sure that Mattiece had ordered the killings. He thought that people were following him. He had decided to hide his copy of the note together with this document in a bank, in case he was killed. He was very frightened.

That was the end of the document.

◆

The thin-faced man watched the car come fast round the corner and park illegally outside the *Post* building. The man and the woman jumped out of the car and ran past him into the building. He had a gun inside his jacket, but it all happened too fast.

◆

Smith Keen and the *Post*'s lawyer, Vincent Litsky, read through Morgan's document. When they had finished, Gray said, 'Well, gentlemen, there's your independent witness. Can we print Darby's story now?'

Keen and Litsky looked at each other. Keen left the office for a few minutes to speak to the newspaper's owner. When he came back he said, 'OK, Gray. We do the story. How long will it take you to write it?'

'I already know the shape of it,' Gray replied. 'I only have to write the details. It should take me about two hours.'

'It's eleven o'clock now,' Keen said. 'Try to finish it by three. Litsky needs time to read it before we print.'

With Darby's help, he finished the story on time. Keen and Litsky read it and made some changes. Darby was watching something out of the window.

'When I've rewritten the story,' Gray said, when Keen and Litsky had finished, 'I have to make some phone calls.'

'We'll be back at half past three,' Keen said.

61

The man and the woman jumped out of the car and ran past him into the building.

'They're outside,' Darby said softly, when Keen and Litsky had left the room.

'Who are?'

'I was watching a man standing on the corner. He looks innocent enough; he's just standing there drinking coffee from a cup. But he's been there a long time – I saw him earlier as well. And just now, when you were talking, I saw the short man who chased me last week come up to the coffee-drinker. They talked for a minute and then the short man disappeared again. They're just waiting for us to leave the building.'

Chapter 17   Time to Trust Someone

The first phone call was to a friend of Grantham at the FBI.

'Phil, this is Gray Grantham. I've got the recorder on.'

'That sounds serious. Go on.'

'We're going to print a story tomorrow about the Rosenberg and Jensen killings. We're going to name Victor Mattiece as the man behind the killings, and also two of his lawyers here in Washington. We'll connect this story with the killing of Verheek in New Orleans. We believe the FBI knew about Mattiece early on but refused to investigate at the request of the White House. We want to give you the chance to comment.' There was silence. 'Phil, are you there?'

'Yes, I think so.'

'Any comment?'

'I'm sure we will have a comment, but I'll have to call you back.'

'OK. I'll look forward to it.'

In fact it was Voyles himself who called back, about ten minutes later. He demanded to speak to Smith Keen.

'What are you doing, Smith?' he said. 'We're still investigating Mattiece. It's too early to be sure. What have you got?'

'Does the name Darby Shaw mean anything to you?' Keen asked.

'Yes.'

'We have the Pelican Brief, Denton, and I'm sitting here looking at Darby Shaw.'

'I was afraid she was dead.'

'No, she's not. And she and Gray Grantham have an independent witness to support the brief. It's a big story, Denton.'

'We need to meet. I'll come round in twenty minutes.'

'OK.'

Keen put the phone down and smiled. He was amused at the idea of the great F. Denton Voyles coming round to his office for a meeting.

The next phone call Gray made was to Fletcher Coal in the White House. Coal agreed that Mattiece had given large amounts of money towards the President's election, but denied that Mattiece and the President were close friends. He had to admit that he was familiar with the Pelican Brief. When Gray asked why there had not been an immediate investigation of Mattiece, Coal angrily denied that the White House had tried to slow down such an investigation.

Then Voyles arrived with K. O. Lewis. Keen took him into his own office and gave him a copy of the story to read while Gray made the third phone call. He rang White and Blazevich and was put through to Marty Velmano. For the third time he explained that he was recording the conversation.

'Mr Velmano,' Gray said, 'we're printing a story in the morning which names your client Victor Mattiece as the man behind the killings of Rosenberg and Jensen.'

'Good!' said Velmano. 'We'll take you to court. By the time we're finished, Mr Mattiece will own the *Washington Post*.'

'Mr Velmano, we have a copy of the Pelican Brief. Have you heard of it?'

Silence.

'We also have a copy of a note you sent to Sims Wakefield on 28 September. In the note you suggested that your client's position would be a lot better without Rosenberg and Jensen on the Supreme Court.'

Silence.

'Mr Velmano, are you there?'

'Yes.'

'We wanted to give you the chance to comment. Do you have any comment?'

'You're going to destroy me,' Velmano said.

◆

Voyles and Lewis entered the room with Smith Keen. Keen introduced them to Darby and Gray. Voyles smiled at Darby and said, 'So you're the one who started all this.'

'No, sir,' she said, 'I think it was Mattiece.'

They sat around a table. Voyles had a piece of paper. He said, 'I'm going to read you something. This is official, and you can use it in your paper. Anything else Lewis or I say is unofficial, and you can't use it. Is that clear?'

Keen and Grantham said yes.

'All right,' Voyles said. 'We received a copy of the Pelican Brief two weeks ago and showed it to the White House on the same day. It was personally delivered by K. O. Lewis to Fletcher Coal. Eric East was also present at the meeting. We thought it was worth investigation, but nothing happened for six days, until Gavin Verheek was murdered in New Orleans. The FBI began a full investigation into Victor Mattiece, involving over four

65

hundred men. We believe Victor Mattiece to be the main suspect in the murders of Rosenberg, Jensen, Thomas Callahan and Verheek, and we are trying to find him.'

'Did the White House interfere with your investigation of Mattiece?' Grantham asked.

'This is now unofficial,' Voyles said. 'You can't use it. OK?'

'OK.'

'Yes, the President asked me not to investigate Mattiece. He said it could be embarrassing to the Government. I recorded the conversation.'

They could hardly believe what they were hearing. He recorded the President!

'I will not allow anyone to hear that recording,' Voyles continued, 'unless the President denies what I have just told you. Anyway, will you use the official story I've given you? Will you put Coal's name there on the front page along with everyone else?'

'Yes, I think he belongs there,' Keen said.

'Good,' said Voyles. 'Can you give me some early copies of the newspaper tomorrow morning? I want to take them round to him myself and watch his face.'

'He'll take the blame,' Keen said. 'It will be the end of his career, but he'll make the President look innocent.'

'Yes, I think you're right,' said Voyles. 'Now, I'd like to speak to Miss Shaw alone, please, if that's all right with her.'

'OK,' she said, 'but Grantham stays.'

'All right.'

When everyone else had left the room, Voyles asked, 'What are you going to do next?'

'First tell me who killed Gavin Verheek,' she said.

'It was Khamel. And Khamel was the one who was shot in the head as you were holding his hand by the river.'

'Who killed him?'

'We think it was someone from the CIA. We know the CIA were investigating Mattiece in a small way. In his oil business Mattiece had connections with some unfriendly Arab countries, so the CIA were already keeping an eye on him. When they saw a copy of the Pelican Brief they sent a few men down to New Orleans to look after you.'

Darby got up and went to the window. It was dark outside now. 'They didn't do a very good job, then,' she said. 'There are men out there now who have been following me for a week or more. One of them chased me in New Orleans, so I don't think he's CIA. Mattiece is so crazy that he'll go on trying to kill me even after he goes to prison – if you catch him.'

'We can help,' Voyles said. 'We can get you out of the country.'

It was time to trust someone. She took a deep breath. 'All right,' she said.

'I'll go and make the arrangements,' Voyles said.

Alone in the room, Darby walked into Gray's arms. 'It's going to be all right now,' he said, holding her. 'It's over. You're safe.'

'I'm going alone, Gray,' she said. 'I'll call you when I'm ready.'

Chapter 18　Away From It All

By 11 p.m. only four lawyers remained in the offices of White and Blazevich. They were Velmano, Sims Wakefield, Jarreld Schwabe and a retired partner named Frank Cortz.

Cortz finished a phone conversation with one of Victor Mattiece's staff. 'That was Strider,' he said. 'They're in Cairo, in some hotel. Mattiece won't talk to us and, of course, he isn't coming back over here. Strider says he's behaving very strangely. They've told the boys with the guns to leave town immediately. The chase is over.'

'So what are we supposed to do?' asked Wakefield.

'We're on our own,' said Cortz. 'Mattiece isn't going to help us.'

There was silence around the table as they all looked into the future. Then Velmano said, 'Grantham only mentioned me and Sims. You two may be O K. And I've got enough money saved to spend the rest of my life hiding in Europe.'

'It's all right for you,' Wakefield said. 'I can't hide. I've got a wife and six children.'

'I think you should go home and tell your wife what to expect,' Velmano said.

'I can't do that,' Wakefield said. He got up and left the room.

A minute later they heard the sound of a single gunshot from his office.

◆

After eight days in the sun of the Virgin Islands her skin was brown enough and her hair was returning to its natural colour. She walked miles up and down the beaches and ate nothing except fish and fruit. She slept a lot the first few days.

She looked at her wrist and then remembered that her watch was in a bag somewhere. She didn't need it here. She woke with the sun and went to bed after dark. But now she was waiting, so she had looked at her wrist.

It was almost dark when the taxi stopped at the end of the small road. He got out, paid the driver and looked at the lights as the car disappeared back up the road. He had one bag. He could see a light from the house between the trees at the edge of the beach, and he walked towards it. He didn't know what to expect. He knew how he felt about her, but did she feel the same?

She was waiting at the back of the house, looking out to sea, with a drink in her hand. She smiled at him, put down her drink and let him come to her.

They kissed for a long minute.

'You're late,' she said.

'This is not the easiest place to find,' Gray said. 'Even when you have directions.'

'I know,' she said. 'That's the idea. It's beautiful, though, isn't it?'

'It is. You are too.'

'Let's go for a walk,' she said.

He changed into a pair of shorts and they walked together on the beach, hand in hand.

'You left early,' she said.

'I got tired of it. I've written a story a day since the big one, and they kept wanting more. I was working eighteen hours a day. Yesterday I said goodbye.'

'I haven't seen a paper for days,' she said.

'Coal's finished. The President will be OK. I don't think he did anything really bad; he's just stupid. He won't get re-elected, though. You read about Wakefield?'

'Yes, that was in the last paper I saw.'

'They've got Schwabe. They want Velmano too, but he's disappeared. Of course Mattiece is in deep trouble, and they're after four of his men too.'

They walked in silence along the beach. She put her arm round his waist and he pulled her closer.

'I've missed you,' she said softly.

He breathed deeply, but said nothing.

'How long will you stay?' she asked.

'I don't know. A couple of weeks. Maybe a year. It depends on you.'

'Let's take it a month at a time. OK, Gray?'

'Perfect.'

ACTIVITIES

Chapters 1–3

Before you read

1 Look at the title of this book.
   a What is a *pelican*? What is a *brief*? What do you think this story is about?
   b *FBI* stands for Federal Bureau of Investigation: The USA's national crime fighting body. *CIA* stands for Central Intelligence Agency: The USA's government organization which investigates political crimes. Do you have similar organizations in your own country?

2 Check these words in your dictionary:
   Constitution environment homosexual
   investigate leak liberal
   Which word means . . .
   a . . . find out more about something.
   b . . . people who love others of the same sex.
   c . . . the laws of a country, taken all together.
   d . . . broad-minded.

3 Choose the right word to complete each sentence:
   a Greenpeace want to protect the natural . . . . . .
   b The newspaper got the story very quickly because it was . . . . . to a reporter by one of the President's men.

After you read

4 Answer these questions:
   a Who is Khamel?
   b How much money is Khamel going to be paid for this job?
   c Why doesn't Judge Rosenberg have guards in his house?
   d How many shots does Khamel fire in Judge Rosenberg's house?
   e How many people are in the Montrose Theatre just before 12.20?
   f What does Khamel use to kill Jensen?

g Who tells the President about the two killings?

h Who is most worried about the murders?

i How does Darby know Thomas Callahan?

j What clues do the FBI find?

k How does Thomas know Gavin?

Chapters 4–6

Before you read

5 What do you think Darby will do if she finds the reason for the two murders?

6 Find these words in your dictionary and check their meanings:

implausible   trace

Write sentences with these groups of words:

a believe/theory/implausible

b trace/phone call/where

After you read

7 Answer these questions:

a What do East and Voyles tell the President about the investigation?

b How would you describe the relationship between Coals and Voyles?

c What has Darby done with the information she found?

d What does Sarge do besides clean the White House?

e Who is Sarge's contact on the *Washington Post*?

f What does Gavin decide to do with Darby's brief?

g Why does someone phone Gray Grantham early in the morning?

h How do the FBI know Khamel was the killer?

i How does Darby's brief get from Gavin to the President?

j Why isn't Darby in the car when it explodes?

k Where does Darby go after the explosion?

l Who does she speak to first?

Chapters 7–10

Before you read

8 What can Darby do to make sure she is safe?

9 Do you think Gavin can help her? Should she trust him?

10 Look these words up in your dictionary:

   client   diskette

   Put the correct word in the spaces in this sentence: The . . . . . was
   handed to him by his . . . . . .

After you read

11 Who says these things? Who to?

   a 'So why don't you leave this one alone and chase the real
      suspects?'

   b 'Patience will get me killed. I've got to keep moving.'

   c 'Suddenly, on Wednesday, Callahan is killed by a car bomb.'

   d 'It will almost be a pity to kill her.

12 Describe the man Darby sees at the hotel's front desk.

13 Answer these questions:

   a Why do the FBI stop investigating the Pelican Brief?

   b How does Gray Grantham get the information he needs to write
      his front page story about Khamel?

   c How does Gavin trace Darby to the Marriott Hotel?

   d Why does Alice Stark go to Darby's flat?

   e Who does Darby recognize at Thomas's funeral?

   f What was strange about Gavin's room when he came out of the
      shower?

14 Croft goes back to the *Washington Post* office after taking the
    photographs of Garcia. Act out the conversation between Croft
    and Gray Grantham.

Chapters 11–14

Before you read

15 What do you think Khamel is going to do next?

16 Who do you think Darby can trust to help her now?

17 Check these words in your dictionary:

acre drilling marsh

Choose the right word to complete each sentence:

a The oilmen set up their machines and were ready to start . . . . . .

b They looked across the . . . . . and out to sea.

c Behind the house was a large garden of more than an . . . . . .

After you read

18 Answer these questions:

a Why does Darby tell Grantham about the Pelican Brief?

b How does Darby realize that the dead man isn't Gavin?

c Why did Voyles record his conversation with the President about the Pelican Brief?

d Where do the CIA lose Darby?

e Where does Darby explain to Gray about Mattiece?

f How does Gray think Garcia is connected to Mattiece?

g Where does Darby go to after New York?

h How does Darby think Mattiece's men knew where Gray was staying?

I How do Darby and Gray trace Garcia?

Chapters 15–18

Before you read

19 What do you think will happen when Gray and Darby find Curtis Morgan?

20 Do you think Mattiece will talk to Matthew Barr? What do you think will happen when they meet?

21 Look in your dictionary for the verb *mug*.

a What do we call the person who commits this crime?

b Where does a mugging usually happen?

c Make a sentence using the verb *mug*.

After you read

22 Answer these questions:

a What is Matthew's opinion of Mattiece?

b How does Sneller trace Darby?

73

c How does Gray find the document written by Morgan?
d Who checks Gray's story?
e Who are the three people Gray telephones?
f Who was most worried by Gray's telephone call?
g Why does Voyles want an early copy of the newspaper?
h How will the FBI help Darby?
i What happens to Sims Wakefield?
j Where do Darby and Gray meet again?

Writing

23 Read Chapters 10 and 11 again. Imagine you are Eric East. Write a report for Denton Voyles about Gavin Verheek's death in New Orleans.

24 Which part of this story do you find most exciting? How does John Grisham keep us reading? Was this a book you 'couldn't put down'?

25 You are a member of Green Rescue. Write an emotional letter to a local paper saying why there must be no drilling for oil in the Louisiana marshes.

26 It is six months after the end of this story. Write another chapter. Say what you think has happened to the characters in this story.

27 The editor at the *Washington Post* wants Gray to come back and work for them again. Write the letter Smith Keen sends him.

28 People's lives can sometimes be ruined by news stories. Are there times when you think journalists should not write a story, even though it is true? Can you think of any examples? How important are journalists in your country?